MEASURING MASTERS

Measuring Length

by Martha E. H. Rustad

PEBBLE
a capstone imprint

Pebble Plus is published by Pebble
1710 Roe Crest Drive, North Mankato,
Minnesota 56003
www.mycapstone.com

Library of Congress Cataloging-in-Publication Data
Library of Congress Cataloging-in-Publication data is available on the Library of Congress website.
ISBN 978-1-9771-0371-0 (library binding)
ISBN 978-1-9771-0556-1 (paperback)
ISBN 978-1-9771-0378-9 (eBook PDF)

Editorial Credits
Michelle Parkin, editor; Elyse White, designer; Heather Mauldin, media researcher;
Laura Manthe, production specialist

Photo Credits
Capstone Studio: Karon Dubke, cover (main image), 17; iStockphoto: akurtz, 21, andresr, 19, ewg3D, 5, OJO Images, 9, Sidekick, 7; Shutterstock: Africa Studio, 15, Marko Poplasen, cover (background), LightField Studios, 11, Ulf Wittrock, 13

Design Elements
Shutterstock: DarkPlatypus, cover

Note to Parents and Teachers

The Measuring Masters set supports national curriculum standards for mathematical practice related to measurement and data. This book describes and illustrates how to measure length. The images support early readers in understanding the text. The repetition of words and phrases helps early readers learn new words. This book also introduces early readers to subject-specific vocabulary words, which are defined in the Glossary section. Early readers may need assistance to read some words and to use the Table of Contents, Glossary, Read More, Internet Sites, Critical Thinking Questions, and Index sections of the book.

Printed and bound in China.
970

Table of Contents

Short or Tall?

We are at the water park!

Am I tall enough to ride the big slide?

Riders must be 48 inches (122 centimeters) tall.

We need to learn how to measure length.

Measuring Tools

A ruler is a stick for measuring.

Lines along the edge mark inches

and centimeters.

A ruler is 12 inches (30 cm) long.

Twelve inches equals 1 foot (30 cm).

A yardstick measures yards.

One yard is 3 feet (0.9 meters) long.

It is the same as 36 inches (91 cm).

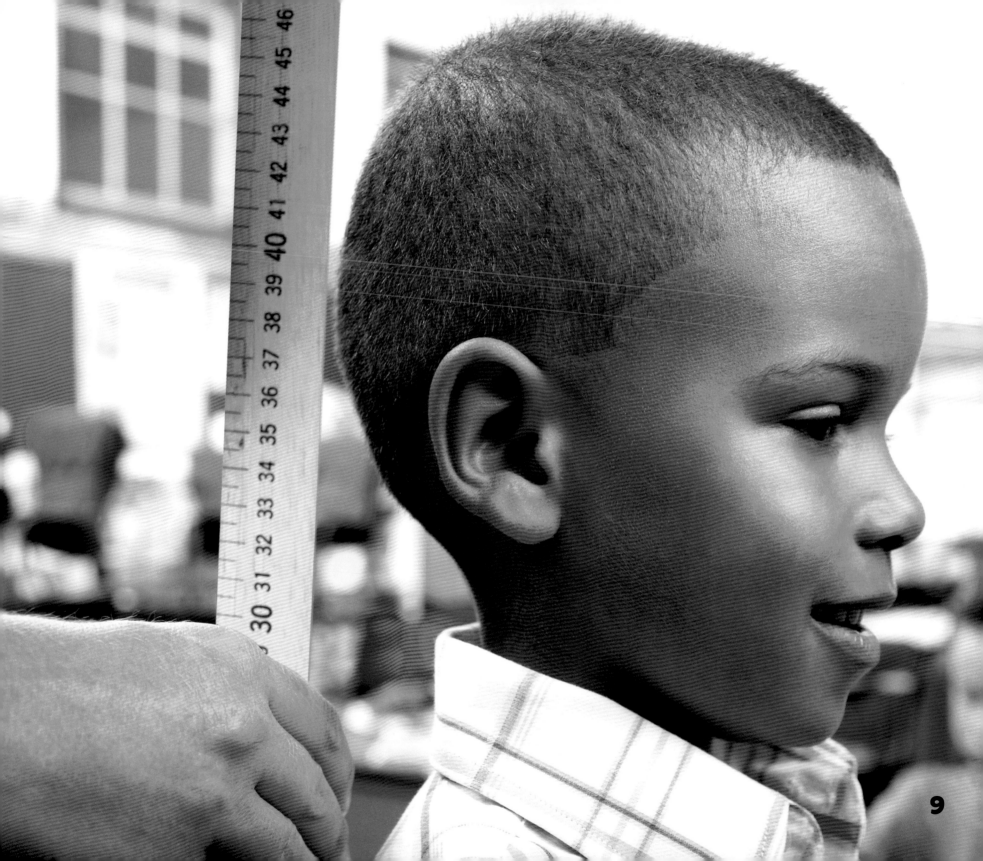

9

A tape measure is a ruler that rolls up.

We use it to measure longer objects.

This one rolls out to 25 feet (7.6 m).

An odometer measures miles.

One mile equals 5,280 feet

(1.6 kilometers).

A car's odometer measures

how far the car goes.

How Long Is It?

I use a ruler to measure short objects.

My pencil is 7 inches (18 cm) long.

The book is 8 inches (20 cm) wide.

I use a yardstick to measure long objects.

The door is 36 inches (91 cm) wide.

My desk is 26.5 inches (67 cm) wide.

I use a tape measure to measure

longer objects.

My dad and I measure the wall.

It is 12 feet (3.7 m) long.

The lifeguard measured me.

I am 4 feet (1.2 m) tall.

That is 48 inches (122 cm).

I can go down the big slide!

Glossary

lifeguard (LIFE-gard)—a person trained to help swimmers

measure (MEZH-ur)—to find the exact amount of something

odometer (oh-DAH-muh-tur)—a tool that measures how far a vehicle has traveled

ruler (ROOL-uhr)—a piece of wood or metal marked with units used for measuring

tape measure (TAYP MEZH-ur)—a long strip of cloth, plastic, or metal marked with units for measuring

yardstick (YARD-stik)—a stick used for measuring; one yard equals 3 feet

Read More

First, Rachel. *Measure It!* Math Beginnings. Minneapolis: Sandcastle, 2016.

Gunderson, Jessica. *How Long?: Wacky Ways to Compare Length.* Wacky Comparisons. North Mankato, Minn.: Picture Window Books, 2014.

Truran, Stacy. *Troy's Tree Fort: Measure Lengths in Standard Units.* Math Masters. New York: PowerKids Press, 2015.

Internet Sites

Use FactHound to find Internet sites related to this book.

Visit *www.facthound.com*

Just type in 9781977103710 and go.

Check out projects, games and lots more at
www.capstonekids.com

Critical Thinking Questions

1. Name an object you could measure with a yardstick.

2. Use a ruler to find the length of your bedroom wall. How long is it?

3. How tall are you? Which tool could you use to find out?

Index